My Adventures
in Online Dating
A Journal

CHRONICLE BOOKS

SAN FRANCISCO

Introduction

Ah, online dating: today's foolproof method for putting out your most authentic self, having completely fantastic romantic dates, and finding the person of your dreams! Right? Well, it's a little more complicated than that. It's tweaking your profile to perfection and sifting through the parade of humanity until you find The One (or at least entertaining yourself with various Mr./Ms. Right Nows in the meantime).

Online dating can feel so ephemeral. This journal is a nice solid way to capture your experiences for future enjoyment and/or cringing.

It's important to present a comprehensive portrait of yourself that's also enjoyable to read. Use the PERSONAL PROFILE questions to plumb your depths and surface those little tidbits that will set you apart from the multitudes on dating sites. The questions in the DATING PROFILE section will help you pinpoint the qualities in a partner that you're looking for, even if it's just someone to have fun with. To liven things up, you can play with the ALTER EGO and CHALLENGE sections.

Use the DATE IDEAS section to think of new and interesting experiences to try with your date. While dinner and a movie are good standbys, dates are great opportunities to expand your horizons. There are studies that suggest if two people go through a novel experience together, they will feel bonded! (This will also get you ahead of the game. Some dating sites ask you to come up with ideas for prospective dates.)

The MEMORABLE MESSAGES section is a great place to write down all the "charming" messages you receive from interested parties. It's fascinating to see how you're perceived by other people through your profile. This section can also be a place to write down all the strange, confusing, but always entertaining messages that come your way. Be sure to capture the truly notable opening lines here.

Use the DATE TRACKER section to help you remember all the details: what you'll tell your friends, and what you might want to keep to yourself. What were your first impressions? Did they match their online profile? Did the conversation go POP POP POPPITY POP or was it awkward? Did you have to make up an emergency to beat a hasty exit, or did the date go on for hours past your bedtimes? Are they a future special someone or just a special friend? Write things down while they are still fresh in your mind. Use the emoji STICKERS to embellish your notes.

Online dating can be a bane or a blessing, but it's a great way to meet a lot of interesting people in short order, and always an adventure.

Personal Profile

Your profile is literally an ad campaign for the brand YOU. Be unique!

WHAT MY FRIENDS WOULD SAY ABOUT ME:

WHAT STRANGERS WOULD NOTICE ABOUT ME:

THREE ADJECTIVES THAT BEST DESCRIBE ME AND WHY. (GIVE EXAMPLES):

WHAT I DO FOR WORK AND FOR FUN:

MY INTERESTS AND HOBBIES:

MY TOP FIVE (BOOKS, MUSIC, TV, MOVIES, FOOD):

THREE THINGS I CAN'T LIVE WITHOUT:

VALUES THAT ARE IMPORTANT TO ME:

ONE RANDOM FACT ABOUT ME:

Alter Ego

Try describing characteristics of your alter ego. Not someone COMPLETELY different, but someone you COULD be. Think about qualities you'd like to develop, activities you'd like to try.

Dating Profile

MY AGE RANGE FOR A MATCH:

WHAT I'M LOOKING FOR RIGHT NOW AND LONG TERM:
(casual sex? serious relationship? marriage? kids?)

MUST-HAVES:

GOOD-TO-HAVES:

DEAL BREAKERS:

Challenge

Try challenging your potential date definitions. Open up your height limit or personality type. Try someone a little younger or a little older. Write down changes you're willing to make.

Date Ideas

Memorable Messages

Memorable Messages

Memorable Messages

DATE TRACKER

DATING SITE / SCREEN NAME:

REAL NAME:

FIRST IMPRESSIONS:

DID THEY MATCH THEIR PROFILE? Y ☐ N ☐ **IF NOT, WHY?**

ONE SENTENCE DESCRIPTION OF DATE:

HIGHLIGHTS:

LOWLIGHTS:

RED FLAGS:

OTHER THOUGHTS:

SEE AGAIN?

☐ OMG YES ☐ HELL NO

NICKNAME TO USE ANONYMOUSLY:

FUTURE POTENTIAL?

☐ FRIEND ☐ FLING ☐ SOUL MATE ☐ NONE OF THE ABOVE

☐ OTHER _____

DATE TRACKER

DATING SITE / SCREEN NAME:

REAL NAME:

FIRST IMPRESSIONS:

DID THEY MATCH THEIR PROFILE? Y ☐ N ☐ IF NOT, WHY?

ONE SENTENCE DESCRIPTION OF DATE:

HIGHLIGHTS:

LOWLIGHTS:

RED FLAGS:

OTHER THOUGHTS:

SEE AGAIN?

☐ OMG YES ☐ HELL NO

NICKNAME TO USE ANONYMOUSLY:

FUTURE POTENTIAL?

☐ FRIEND ☐ FLING ☐ SOUL MATE ☐ NONE OF THE ABOVE

☐ OTHER _____

DATE TRACKER

DATING SITE / SCREEN NAME:

REAL NAME:

FIRST IMPRESSIONS:

DID THEY MATCH THEIR PROFILE? Y ☐ N ☐ **IF NOT, WHY?**

ONE SENTENCE DESCRIPTION OF DATE:

HIGHLIGHTS:

LOWLIGHTS:

RED FLAGS:

OTHER THOUGHTS:

SEE AGAIN?

☐ OMG YES   ☐ HELL NO

NICKNAME TO USE ANONYMOUSLY:

FUTURE POTENTIAL?

☐ FRIEND   ☐ FLING   ☐ SOUL MATE   ☐ NONE OF THE ABOVE

☐ OTHER _____

DATE TRACKER

DATING SITE / SCREEN NAME:

REAL NAME:

FIRST IMPRESSIONS:

DID THEY MATCH THEIR PROFILE? Y ☐ N ☐ IF NOT, WHY?

ONE SENTENCE DESCRIPTION OF DATE:

HIGHLIGHTS:

LOWLIGHTS:

RED FLAGS:

OTHER THOUGHTS:

SEE AGAIN?

☐ OMG YES ☐ HELL NO

NICKNAME TO USE ANONYMOUSLY:

FUTURE POTENTIAL?

☐ FRIEND ☐ FLING ☐ SOUL MATE ☐ NONE OF THE ABOVE

☐ OTHER _____

DATE TRACKER

DATING SITE / SCREEN NAME:

REAL NAME:

FIRST IMPRESSIONS:

DID THEY MATCH THEIR PROFILE? Y ☐ N ☐ IF NOT, WHY?

ONE SENTENCE DESCRIPTION OF DATE:

HIGHLIGHTS:

LOWLIGHTS:

RED FLAGS:

OTHER THOUGHTS:

SEE AGAIN?

☐ OMG YES ☐ HELL NO

NICKNAME TO USE ANONYMOUSLY:

FUTURE POTENTIAL?

☐ FRIEND ☐ FLING ☐ SOUL MATE ☐ NONE OF THE ABOVE

☐ OTHER _____

DATE TRACKER

DATING SITE / SCREEN NAME:

REAL NAME:

FIRST IMPRESSIONS:

DID THEY MATCH THEIR PROFILE? Y ☐ N ☐ IF NOT, WHY?

ONE SENTENCE DESCRIPTION OF DATE:

HIGHLIGHTS:

LOWLIGHTS:

RED FLAGS:

OTHER THOUGHTS:

SEE AGAIN?

☐ OMG YES ☐ HELL NO

NICKNAME TO USE ANONYMOUSLY:

FUTURE POTENTIAL?

☐ FRIEND ☐ FLING ☐ SOUL MATE ☐ NONE OF THE ABOVE

☐ OTHER _____

DATE TRACKER

DATING SITE / SCREEN NAME:

REAL NAME:

FIRST IMPRESSIONS:

DID THEY MATCH THEIR PROFILE? Y ☐ N ☐ IF NOT, WHY?

ONE SENTENCE DESCRIPTION OF DATE:

HIGHLIGHTS:

LOWLIGHTS:

RED FLAGS:

OTHER THOUGHTS:

SEE AGAIN?

☐ OMG YES ☐ HELL NO

NICKNAME TO USE ANONYMOUSLY:

FUTURE POTENTIAL?

☐ FRIEND ☐ FLING ☐ SOUL MATE ☐ NONE OF THE ABOVE

☐ OTHER _____

DATE TRACKER

DATING SITE / SCREEN NAME:

REAL NAME:

FIRST IMPRESSIONS:

DID THEY MATCH THEIR PROFILE? Y ☐ N ☐ IF NOT, WHY?

ONE SENTENCE DESCRIPTION OF DATE:

HIGHLIGHTS:

LOWLIGHTS:

RED FLAGS:

OTHER THOUGHTS:

SEE AGAIN?

☐ OMG YES ☐ HELL NO

NICKNAME TO USE ANONYMOUSLY:

FUTURE POTENTIAL?

☐ FRIEND ☐ FLING ☐ SOUL MATE ☐ NONE OF THE ABOVE

☐ OTHER _____

DATE TRACKER

DATING SITE / SCREEN NAME:

REAL NAME:

FIRST IMPRESSIONS:

DID THEY MATCH THEIR PROFILE? Y ☐ N ☐ **IF NOT, WHY?**

ONE SENTENCE DESCRIPTION OF DATE:

HIGHLIGHTS:

LOWLIGHTS:

RED FLAGS:

OTHER THOUGHTS:

SEE AGAIN?

☐ OMG YES ☐ HELL NO

NICKNAME TO USE ANONYMOUSLY:

FUTURE POTENTIAL?

☐ FRIEND ☐ FLING ☐ SOUL MATE ☐ NONE OF THE ABOVE

☐ OTHER _____

DATE TRACKER

DATING SITE / SCREEN NAME:

REAL NAME:

FIRST IMPRESSIONS:

DID THEY MATCH THEIR PROFILE? Y ☐ N ☐ IF NOT, WHY?

ONE SENTENCE DESCRIPTION OF DATE:

HIGHLIGHTS:

LOWLIGHTS:

RED FLAGS:

OTHER THOUGHTS:

SEE AGAIN?

☐ OMG YES ☐ HELL NO

NICKNAME TO USE ANONYMOUSLY:

FUTURE POTENTIAL?

☐ FRIEND ☐ FLING ☐ SOUL MATE ☐ NONE OF THE ABOVE

☐ OTHER _____

DATE TRACKER

DATING SITE / SCREEN NAME:

REAL NAME:

FIRST IMPRESSIONS:

DID THEY MATCH THEIR PROFILE? Y ☐ N ☐ IF NOT, WHY?

ONE SENTENCE DESCRIPTION OF DATE:

HIGHLIGHTS:

LOWLIGHTS:

RED FLAGS:

OTHER THOUGHTS:

SEE AGAIN?

☐ OMG YES ☐ HELL NO

NICKNAME TO USE ANONYMOUSLY:

FUTURE POTENTIAL?

☐ FRIEND ☐ FLING ☐ SOUL MATE ☐ NONE OF THE ABOVE

☐ OTHER _____

DATE TRACKER

DATING SITE / SCREEN NAME:

REAL NAME:

FIRST IMPRESSIONS:

DID THEY MATCH THEIR PROFILE? Y ☐ N ☐ IF NOT, WHY?

ONE SENTENCE DESCRIPTION OF DATE:

HIGHLIGHTS:

LOWLIGHTS:

RED FLAGS:

OTHER THOUGHTS:

SEE AGAIN?

☐ OMG YES ☐ HELL NO

NICKNAME TO USE ANONYMOUSLY:

FUTURE POTENTIAL?

☐ FRIEND ☐ FLING ☐ SOUL MATE ☐ NONE OF THE ABOVE

☐ OTHER _____

DATE TRACKER

DATING SITE / SCREEN NAME:

REAL NAME:

FIRST IMPRESSIONS:

DID THEY MATCH THEIR PROFILE? Y ☐ N ☐ IF NOT, WHY?

ONE SENTENCE DESCRIPTION OF DATE:

HIGHLIGHTS:

LOWLIGHTS:

RED FLAGS:

OTHER THOUGHTS:

SEE AGAIN?

☐ OMG YES   ☐ HELL NO

NICKNAME TO USE ANONYMOUSLY:

FUTURE POTENTIAL?

☐ FRIEND   ☐ FLING   ☐ SOUL MATE   ☐ NONE OF THE ABOVE

☐ OTHER _____

DATE TRACKER

DATING SITE / SCREEN NAME:

REAL NAME:

FIRST IMPRESSIONS:

DID THEY MATCH THEIR PROFILE? Y ☐ N ☐ IF NOT, WHY?

ONE SENTENCE DESCRIPTION OF DATE:

HIGHLIGHTS:

LOWLIGHTS:

RED FLAGS:

OTHER THOUGHTS:

SEE AGAIN?

☐ OMG YES   ☐ HELL NO

NICKNAME TO USE ANONYMOUSLY:

FUTURE POTENTIAL?

☐ FRIEND   ☐ FLING   ☐ SOUL MATE   ☐ NONE OF THE ABOVE

☐ OTHER _____

DATE TRACKER

DATING SITE / SCREEN NAME:

REAL NAME:

FIRST IMPRESSIONS:

DID THEY MATCH THEIR PROFILE? Y ☐ N ☐ IF NOT, WHY?

ONE SENTENCE DESCRIPTION OF DATE:

HIGHLIGHTS:

LOWLIGHTS:

RED FLAGS:

OTHER THOUGHTS:

SEE AGAIN?

☐ OMG YES   ☐ HELL NO

NICKNAME TO USE ANONYMOUSLY:

FUTURE POTENTIAL?

☐ FRIEND   ☐ FLING   ☐ SOUL MATE   ☐ NONE OF THE ABOVE

☐ OTHER _____

DATE TRACKER

DATING SITE / SCREEN NAME:

REAL NAME:

FIRST IMPRESSIONS:

DID THEY MATCH THEIR PROFILE? Y ☐ N ☐ IF NOT, WHY?

ONE SENTENCE DESCRIPTION OF DATE:

HIGHLIGHTS:

LOWLIGHTS:

RED FLAGS:

OTHER THOUGHTS:

SEE AGAIN?

☐ OMG YES ☐ HELL NO

NICKNAME TO USE ANONYMOUSLY:

FUTURE POTENTIAL?

☐ FRIEND ☐ FLING ☐ SOUL MATE ☐ NONE OF THE ABOVE

☐ OTHER _____

DATE TRACKER

DATING SITE / SCREEN NAME:

REAL NAME:

FIRST IMPRESSIONS:

DID THEY MATCH THEIR PROFILE? Y ☐ N ☐ IF NOT, WHY?

ONE SENTENCE DESCRIPTION OF DATE:

HIGHLIGHTS:

LOWLIGHTS:

RED FLAGS:

OTHER THOUGHTS:

SEE AGAIN?

☐ OMG YES ☐ HELL NO

NICKNAME TO USE ANONYMOUSLY:

FUTURE POTENTIAL?

☐ FRIEND ☐ FLING ☐ SOUL MATE ☐ NONE OF THE ABOVE

☐ OTHER _____

DATE TRACKER

DATING SITE / SCREEN NAME:

REAL NAME:

FIRST IMPRESSIONS:

DID THEY MATCH THEIR PROFILE? Y ☐ N ☐ IF NOT, WHY?

ONE SENTENCE DESCRIPTION OF DATE:

HIGHLIGHTS:

LOWLIGHTS:

RED FLAGS:

OTHER THOUGHTS:

SEE AGAIN?

☐ OMG YES ☐ HELL NO

NICKNAME TO USE ANONYMOUSLY:

FUTURE POTENTIAL?

☐ FRIEND ☐ FLING ☐ SOUL MATE ☐ NONE OF THE ABOVE

☐ OTHER _____

DATE TRACKER

DATING SITE / SCREEN NAME:

REAL NAME:

FIRST IMPRESSIONS:

DID THEY MATCH THEIR PROFILE? Y ☐ N ☐ IF NOT, WHY?

ONE SENTENCE DESCRIPTION OF DATE:

HIGHLIGHTS:

LOWLIGHTS:

RED FLAGS:

OTHER THOUGHTS:

SEE AGAIN?

☐ OMG YES ☐ HELL NO

NICKNAME TO USE ANONYMOUSLY:

FUTURE POTENTIAL?

☐ FRIEND ☐ FLING ☐ SOUL MATE ☐ NONE OF THE ABOVE

☐ OTHER _____

DATE TRACKER

DATING SITE / SCREEN NAME:

REAL NAME:

FIRST IMPRESSIONS:

DID THEY MATCH THEIR PROFILE? Y ☐ N ☐ IF NOT, WHY?

ONE SENTENCE DESCRIPTION OF DATE:

HIGHLIGHTS:

LOWLIGHTS:

RED FLAGS:

OTHER THOUGHTS:

SEE AGAIN?

☐ OMG YES ☐ HELL NO

NICKNAME TO USE ANONYMOUSLY:

FUTURE POTENTIAL?

☐ FRIEND ☐ FLING ☐ SOUL MATE ☐ NONE OF THE ABOVE

☐ OTHER _____

DATE TRACKER

DATING SITE / SCREEN NAME:

REAL NAME:

FIRST IMPRESSIONS:

DID THEY MATCH THEIR PROFILE? Y ☐ N ☐ IF NOT, WHY?

ONE SENTENCE DESCRIPTION OF DATE:

HIGHLIGHTS:

LOWLIGHTS:

RED FLAGS:

OTHER THOUGHTS:

SEE AGAIN?

☐ OMG YES ☐ HELL NO

NICKNAME TO USE ANONYMOUSLY:

FUTURE POTENTIAL?

☐ FRIEND ☐ FLING ☐ SOUL MATE ☐ NONE OF THE ABOVE

☐ OTHER _____

DATE TRACKER

DATING SITE / SCREEN NAME:

REAL NAME:

FIRST IMPRESSIONS:

DID THEY MATCH THEIR PROFILE? Y ☐ N ☐ **IF NOT, WHY?**

ONE SENTENCE DESCRIPTION OF DATE:

HIGHLIGHTS:

LOWLIGHTS:

RED FLAGS:

OTHER THOUGHTS:

SEE AGAIN?

☐ OMG YES ☐ HELL NO

NICKNAME TO USE ANONYMOUSLY:

FUTURE POTENTIAL?

☐ FRIEND ☐ FLING ☐ SOUL MATE ☐ NONE OF THE ABOVE

☐ OTHER _____

DATE TRACKER

DATING SITE / SCREEN NAME:

REAL NAME:

FIRST IMPRESSIONS:

DID THEY MATCH THEIR PROFILE? Y ☐ N ☐ **IF NOT, WHY?**

ONE SENTENCE DESCRIPTION OF DATE:

HIGHLIGHTS:

LOWLIGHTS:

RED FLAGS:

OTHER THOUGHTS:

SEE AGAIN?

☐ OMG YES ☐ HELL NO

NICKNAME TO USE ANONYMOUSLY:

FUTURE POTENTIAL?

☐ FRIEND ☐ FLING ☐ SOUL MATE ☐ NONE OF THE ABOVE

☐ OTHER _____

DATE TRACKER

DATING SITE / SCREEN NAME:

REAL NAME:

FIRST IMPRESSIONS:

DID THEY MATCH THEIR PROFILE? Y ☐ N ☐ IF NOT, WHY?

ONE SENTENCE DESCRIPTION OF DATE:

HIGHLIGHTS:

LOWLIGHTS:

RED FLAGS:

OTHER THOUGHTS:

SEE AGAIN?

☐ OMG YES ☐ HELL NO

NICKNAME TO USE ANONYMOUSLY:

FUTURE POTENTIAL?

☐ FRIEND ☐ FLING ☐ SOUL MATE ☐ NONE OF THE ABOVE

☐ OTHER _____

DATE TRACKER

DATING SITE / SCREEN NAME:

REAL NAME:

FIRST IMPRESSIONS:

DID THEY MATCH THEIR PROFILE? Y ☐ N ☐ IF NOT, WHY?

ONE SENTENCE DESCRIPTION OF DATE:

HIGHLIGHTS:

LOWLIGHTS:

RED FLAGS:

OTHER THOUGHTS:

SEE AGAIN?

☐ OMG YES ☐ HELL NO

NICKNAME TO USE ANONYMOUSLY:

FUTURE POTENTIAL?

☐ FRIEND ☐ FLING ☐ SOUL MATE ☐ NONE OF THE ABOVE

☐ OTHER _____

DATE TRACKER

DATING SITE / SCREEN NAME:

REAL NAME:

FIRST IMPRESSIONS:

DID THEY MATCH THEIR PROFILE? Y ☐ N ☐ IF NOT, WHY?

ONE SENTENCE DESCRIPTION OF DATE:

HIGHLIGHTS:

LOWLIGHTS:

RED FLAGS:

OTHER THOUGHTS:

SEE AGAIN?

☐ OMG YES ☐ HELL NO

NICKNAME TO USE ANONYMOUSLY:

FUTURE POTENTIAL?

☐ FRIEND ☐ FLING ☐ SOUL MATE ☐ NONE OF THE ABOVE

☐ OTHER _____

DATE TRACKER

DATING SITE / SCREEN NAME:

REAL NAME:

FIRST IMPRESSIONS:

DID THEY MATCH THEIR PROFILE? Y ☐ N ☐ IF NOT, WHY?

ONE SENTENCE DESCRIPTION OF DATE:

HIGHLIGHTS:

LOWLIGHTS:

RED FLAGS:

OTHER THOUGHTS:

SEE AGAIN?

☐ OMG YES ☐ HELL NO

NICKNAME TO USE ANONYMOUSLY:

FUTURE POTENTIAL?

☐ FRIEND ☐ FLING ☐ SOUL MATE ☐ NONE OF THE ABOVE

☐ OTHER _____

DATE TRACKER

DATING SITE / SCREEN NAME:

REAL NAME:

FIRST IMPRESSIONS:

DID THEY MATCH THEIR PROFILE? Y ☐ N ☐ IF NOT, WHY?

ONE SENTENCE DESCRIPTION OF DATE:

HIGHLIGHTS:

LOWLIGHTS:

RED FLAGS:

OTHER THOUGHTS:

SEE AGAIN?

☐ OMG YES ☐ HELL NO

NICKNAME TO USE ANONYMOUSLY:

FUTURE POTENTIAL?

☐ FRIEND ☐ FLING ☐ SOUL MATE ☐ NONE OF THE ABOVE

☐ OTHER _____

DATE TRACKER

DATING SITE / SCREEN NAME:

REAL NAME:

FIRST IMPRESSIONS:

DID THEY MATCH THEIR PROFILE? Y ☐ N ☐ IF NOT, WHY?

ONE SENTENCE DESCRIPTION OF DATE:

HIGHLIGHTS:

LOWLIGHTS:

RED FLAGS:

OTHER THOUGHTS:

SEE AGAIN?

☐ OMG YES ☐ HELL NO

NICKNAME TO USE ANONYMOUSLY:

FUTURE POTENTIAL?

☐ FRIEND ☐ FLING ☐ SOUL MATE ☐ NONE OF THE ABOVE

☐ OTHER _____

DATE TRACKER

DATING SITE / SCREEN NAME:

REAL NAME:

FIRST IMPRESSIONS:

DID THEY MATCH THEIR PROFILE? Y ☐ N ☐ **IF NOT, WHY?**

ONE SENTENCE DESCRIPTION OF DATE:

HIGHLIGHTS:

LOWLIGHTS:

RED FLAGS:

OTHER THOUGHTS:

SEE AGAIN?

☐ OMG YES ☐ HELL NO

NICKNAME TO USE ANONYMOUSLY:

FUTURE POTENTIAL?

☐ FRIEND ☐ FLING ☐ SOUL MATE ☐ NONE OF THE ABOVE

☐ OTHER _____

DATE TRACKER

DATING SITE / SCREEN NAME:

REAL NAME:

FIRST IMPRESSIONS:

DID THEY MATCH THEIR PROFILE? Y ☐ N ☐ IF NOT, WHY?

ONE SENTENCE DESCRIPTION OF DATE:

HIGHLIGHTS:

LOWLIGHTS:

RED FLAGS:

OTHER THOUGHTS:

SEE AGAIN?

□ OMG YES   □ HELL NO

NICKNAME TO USE ANONYMOUSLY:

FUTURE POTENTIAL?

□ FRIEND   □ FLING   □ SOUL MATE   □ NONE OF THE ABOVE

□ OTHER _____

DATE TRACKER

DATING SITE / SCREEN NAME:

REAL NAME:

FIRST IMPRESSIONS:

DID THEY MATCH THEIR PROFILE? Y ☐ N ☐ IF NOT, WHY?

ONE SENTENCE DESCRIPTION OF DATE:

HIGHLIGHTS:

LOWLIGHTS:

RED FLAGS:

OTHER THOUGHTS:

SEE AGAIN?

☐ OMG YES   ☐ HELL NO

NICKNAME TO USE ANONYMOUSLY:

FUTURE POTENTIAL?

☐ FRIEND   ☐ FLING   ☐ SOUL MATE   ☐ NONE OF THE ABOVE

☐ OTHER _____

DATE TRACKER

DATING SITE / SCREEN NAME:

REAL NAME:

FIRST IMPRESSIONS:

DID THEY MATCH THEIR PROFILE? Y ☐ N ☐ IF NOT, WHY?

ONE SENTENCE DESCRIPTION OF DATE:

HIGHLIGHTS:

LOWLIGHTS:

RED FLAGS:

OTHER THOUGHTS:

SEE AGAIN?

☐ OMG YES ☐ HELL NO

NICKNAME TO USE ANONYMOUSLY:

FUTURE POTENTIAL?

☐ FRIEND ☐ FLING ☐ SOUL MATE ☐ NONE OF THE ABOVE

☐ OTHER _____

DATE TRACKER

DATING SITE / SCREEN NAME:

REAL NAME:

FIRST IMPRESSIONS:

DID THEY MATCH THEIR PROFILE? Y ☐ N ☐ IF NOT, WHY?

ONE SENTENCE DESCRIPTION OF DATE:

HIGHLIGHTS:

LOWLIGHTS:

RED FLAGS:

OTHER THOUGHTS:

SEE AGAIN?

☐ OMG YES ☐ HELL NO

NICKNAME TO USE ANONYMOUSLY:

FUTURE POTENTIAL?

☐ FRIEND ☐ FLING ☐ SOUL MATE ☐ NONE OF THE ABOVE

☐ OTHER _____

DATE TRACKER

DATING SITE / SCREEN NAME:

REAL NAME:

FIRST IMPRESSIONS:

DID THEY MATCH THEIR PROFILE? Y ☐ N ☐ IF NOT, WHY?

ONE SENTENCE DESCRIPTION OF DATE:

HIGHLIGHTS:

LOWLIGHTS:

RED FLAGS:

OTHER THOUGHTS:

SEE AGAIN?

☐ OMG YES   ☐ HELL NO

NICKNAME TO USE ANONYMOUSLY:

FUTURE POTENTIAL?

☐ FRIEND   ☐ FLING   ☐ SOUL MATE   ☐ NONE OF THE ABOVE

☐ OTHER _____

DATE TRACKER

DATING SITE / SCREEN NAME:

REAL NAME:

FIRST IMPRESSIONS:

DID THEY MATCH THEIR PROFILE? Y ☐ N ☐ IF NOT, WHY?

ONE SENTENCE DESCRIPTION OF DATE:

HIGHLIGHTS:

LOWLIGHTS:

RED FLAGS:

OTHER THOUGHTS:

SEE AGAIN?

☐ OMG YES ☐ HELL NO

NICKNAME TO USE ANONYMOUSLY:

FUTURE POTENTIAL?

☐ FRIEND ☐ FLING ☐ SOUL MATE ☐ NONE OF THE ABOVE

☐ OTHER _____

DATE TRACKER

DATING SITE / SCREEN NAME:

REAL NAME:

FIRST IMPRESSIONS:

DID THEY MATCH THEIR PROFILE? Y ☐ N ☐ IF NOT, WHY?

ONE SENTENCE DESCRIPTION OF DATE:

HIGHLIGHTS:

LOWLIGHTS:

RED FLAGS:

OTHER THOUGHTS:

SEE AGAIN?

☐ OMG YES ☐ HELL NO

NICKNAME TO USE ANONYMOUSLY:

FUTURE POTENTIAL?

☐ FRIEND ☐ FLING ☐ SOUL MATE ☐ NONE OF THE ABOVE

☐ OTHER _____

DATE TRACKER

DATING SITE / SCREEN NAME:

REAL NAME:

FIRST IMPRESSIONS:

DID THEY MATCH THEIR PROFILE? Y ☐ N ☐ IF NOT, WHY?

ONE SENTENCE DESCRIPTION OF DATE:

HIGHLIGHTS:

LOWLIGHTS:

RED FLAGS:

OTHER THOUGHTS:

SEE AGAIN?

☐ OMG YES ☐ HELL NO

NICKNAME TO USE ANONYMOUSLY:

FUTURE POTENTIAL?

☐ FRIEND ☐ FLING ☐ SOUL MATE ☐ NONE OF THE ABOVE

☐ OTHER _____

DATE TRACKER

DATING SITE / SCREEN NAME:

REAL NAME:

FIRST IMPRESSIONS:

DID THEY MATCH THEIR PROFILE? Y ☐ N ☐ IF NOT, WHY?

ONE SENTENCE DESCRIPTION OF DATE:

HIGHLIGHTS:

LOWLIGHTS:

RED FLAGS:

OTHER THOUGHTS:

SEE AGAIN?

☐ OMG YES ☐ HELL NO

NICKNAME TO USE ANONYMOUSLY:

FUTURE POTENTIAL?

☐ FRIEND ☐ FLING ☐ SOUL MATE ☐ NONE OF THE ABOVE

☐ OTHER _____

DATE TRACKER

DATING SITE / SCREEN NAME:

REAL NAME:

FIRST IMPRESSIONS:

DID THEY MATCH THEIR PROFILE? Y ☐ N ☐ IF NOT, WHY?

ONE SENTENCE DESCRIPTION OF DATE:

HIGHLIGHTS:

LOWLIGHTS:

RED FLAGS:

OTHER THOUGHTS:

SEE AGAIN?

☐ OMG YES ☐ HELL NO

NICKNAME TO USE ANONYMOUSLY:

FUTURE POTENTIAL?

☐ FRIEND ☐ FLING ☐ SOUL MATE ☐ NONE OF THE ABOVE

☐ OTHER _____

DATE TRACKER

DATING SITE / SCREEN NAME:

REAL NAME:

FIRST IMPRESSIONS:

DID THEY MATCH THEIR PROFILE? Y ☐ N ☐ IF NOT, WHY?

ONE SENTENCE DESCRIPTION OF DATE:

HIGHLIGHTS:

LOWLIGHTS:

RED FLAGS:

OTHER THOUGHTS:

SEE AGAIN?

☐ OMG YES ☐ HELL NO

NICKNAME TO USE ANONYMOUSLY:

FUTURE POTENTIAL?

☐ FRIEND ☐ FLING ☐ SOUL MATE ☐ NONE OF THE ABOVE

☐ OTHER _____

DATE TRACKER

DATING SITE / SCREEN NAME:

REAL NAME:

FIRST IMPRESSIONS:

DID THEY MATCH THEIR PROFILE? Y ☐ N ☐ IF NOT, WHY?

ONE SENTENCE DESCRIPTION OF DATE:

HIGHLIGHTS:

LOWLIGHTS:

RED FLAGS:

OTHER THOUGHTS:

SEE AGAIN?

☐ OMG YES ☐ HELL NO

NICKNAME TO USE ANONYMOUSLY:

FUTURE POTENTIAL?

☐ FRIEND ☐ FLING ☐ SOUL MATE ☐ NONE OF THE ABOVE

☐ OTHER _____

DATE TRACKER

DATING SITE / SCREEN NAME:

REAL NAME:

FIRST IMPRESSIONS:

DID THEY MATCH THEIR PROFILE? Y □ N □ IF NOT, WHY?

ONE SENTENCE DESCRIPTION OF DATE:

HIGHLIGHTS:

LOWLIGHTS:

RED FLAGS:

OTHER THOUGHTS:

SEE AGAIN?

☐ OMG YES   ☐ HELL NO

NICKNAME TO USE ANONYMOUSLY:

FUTURE POTENTIAL?

☐ FRIEND ☐ FLING ☐ SOUL MATE ☐ NONE OF THE ABOVE

☐ OTHER _____

DATE TRACKER

DATING SITE / SCREEN NAME:

REAL NAME:

FIRST IMPRESSIONS:

DID THEY MATCH THEIR PROFILE? Y ☐ N ☐ IF NOT, WHY?

ONE SENTENCE DESCRIPTION OF DATE:

HIGHLIGHTS:

LOWLIGHTS:

RED FLAGS:

OTHER THOUGHTS:

SEE AGAIN?

☐ OMG YES ☐ HELL NO

NICKNAME TO USE ANONYMOUSLY:

FUTURE POTENTIAL?

☐ FRIEND ☐ FLING ☐ SOUL MATE ☐ NONE OF THE ABOVE

☐ OTHER _____

DATE TRACKER

DATING SITE / SCREEN NAME:

REAL NAME:

FIRST IMPRESSIONS:

DID THEY MATCH THEIR PROFILE? Y ☐ N ☐ IF NOT, WHY?

ONE SENTENCE DESCRIPTION OF DATE:

HIGHLIGHTS:

LOWLIGHTS:

RED FLAGS:

OTHER THOUGHTS:

SEE AGAIN?

☐ OMG YES   ☐ HELL NO

NICKNAME TO USE ANONYMOUSLY:

FUTURE POTENTIAL?

☐ FRIEND ☐ FLING ☐ SOUL MATE ☐ NONE OF THE ABOVE

☐ OTHER _____

DATE TRACKER

DATING SITE / SCREEN NAME:

REAL NAME:

FIRST IMPRESSIONS:

DID THEY MATCH THEIR PROFILE? Y ☐ N ☐ IF NOT, WHY?

ONE SENTENCE DESCRIPTION OF DATE:

HIGHLIGHTS:

LOWLIGHTS:

RED FLAGS:

OTHER THOUGHTS:

SEE AGAIN?

☐ OMG YES ☐ HELL NO

NICKNAME TO USE ANONYMOUSLY:

FUTURE POTENTIAL?

☐ FRIEND ☐ FLING ☐ SOUL MATE ☐ NONE OF THE ABOVE

☐ OTHER _____

DATE TRACKER

DATING SITE / SCREEN NAME:

REAL NAME:

FIRST IMPRESSIONS:

DID THEY MATCH THEIR PROFILE? Y ☐ N ☐ IF NOT, WHY?

ONE SENTENCE DESCRIPTION OF DATE:

HIGHLIGHTS:

LOWLIGHTS:

RED FLAGS:

OTHER THOUGHTS:

SEE AGAIN?

☐ OMG YES ☐ HELL NO

NICKNAME TO USE ANONYMOUSLY:

FUTURE POTENTIAL?

☐ FRIEND ☐ FLING ☐ SOUL MATE ☐ NONE OF THE ABOVE

☐ OTHER _____

DATE TRACKER

DATING SITE / SCREEN NAME:

REAL NAME:

FIRST IMPRESSIONS:

DID THEY MATCH THEIR PROFILE? Y ☐ N ☐ IF NOT, WHY?

ONE SENTENCE DESCRIPTION OF DATE:

HIGHLIGHTS:

LOWLIGHTS:

RED FLAGS:

OTHER THOUGHTS:

SEE AGAIN?

☐ OMG YES ☐ HELL NO

NICKNAME TO USE ANONYMOUSLY:

FUTURE POTENTIAL?

☐ FRIEND ☐ FLING ☐ SOUL MATE ☐ NONE OF THE ABOVE

☐ OTHER _____

DATE TRACKER

DATING SITE / SCREEN NAME:

REAL NAME:

FIRST IMPRESSIONS:

DID THEY MATCH THEIR PROFILE? Y ☐ N ☐ IF NOT, WHY?

ONE SENTENCE DESCRIPTION OF DATE:

HIGHLIGHTS:

LOWLIGHTS:

RED FLAGS:

OTHER THOUGHTS:

SEE AGAIN?

☐ OMG YES ☐ HELL NO

NICKNAME TO USE ANONYMOUSLY:

FUTURE POTENTIAL?

☐ FRIEND ☐ FLING ☐ SOUL MATE ☐ NONE OF THE ABOVE

☐ OTHER _____

DATE TRACKER

DATING SITE / SCREEN NAME:

REAL NAME:

FIRST IMPRESSIONS:

DID THEY MATCH THEIR PROFILE? Y ☐ N ☐ IF NOT, WHY?

ONE SENTENCE DESCRIPTION OF DATE:

HIGHLIGHTS:

LOWLIGHTS:

RED FLAGS:

OTHER THOUGHTS:

SEE AGAIN?

☐ OMG YES ☐ HELL NO

NICKNAME TO USE ANONYMOUSLY:

FUTURE POTENTIAL?

☐ FRIEND ☐ FLING ☐ SOUL MATE ☐ NONE OF THE ABOVE

☐ OTHER _____

DATE TRACKER

DATING SITE / SCREEN NAME:

REAL NAME:

FIRST IMPRESSIONS:

DID THEY MATCH THEIR PROFILE? Y ☐ N ☐ IF NOT, WHY?

ONE SENTENCE DESCRIPTION OF DATE:

HIGHLIGHTS:

LOWLIGHTS:

RED FLAGS:

OTHER THOUGHTS:

SEE AGAIN?

☐ OMG YES ☐ HELL NO

NICKNAME TO USE ANONYMOUSLY:

FUTURE POTENTIAL?

☐ FRIEND ☐ FLING ☐ SOUL MATE ☐ NONE OF THE ABOVE

☐ OTHER _____

Notes

ISBN 978-1-4521-2889-4

Manufactured in China

MIX
Paper from
responsible sources
FSC™ C006948

Design and Illustrations by Sally Carmichael
Typeset in Campton

Chronicle Books publishes distinctive books and
gifts. From award-winning children's titles, bestselling
cookbooks, and eclectic pop culture to acclaimed
works of art and design, stationery, and journals, we
craft publishing that's instantly recognizable for its
spirit and creativity. Enjoy our publishing and become
part of our community at www.chroniclebooks.com.

10 9 8 7 6 5 4 3 2 1

Chronicle Books LLC
680 Second Street
San Francisco, CA 94107
www.chroniclebooks.com

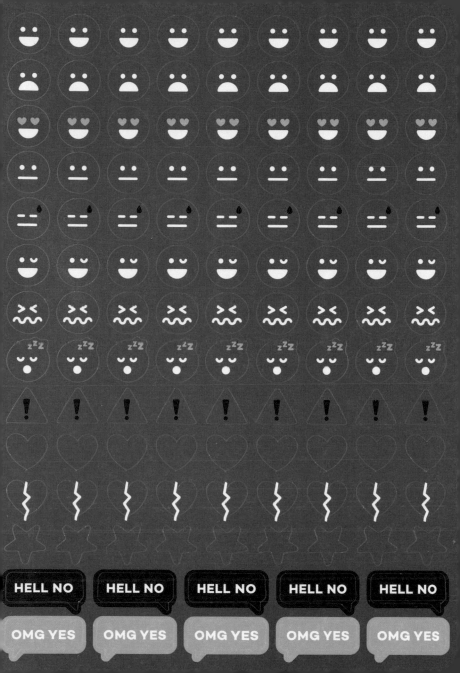